ALL LOVELY THINGS

A FIELD JOURNAL FOR THE OBJECTS THAT DEFINE US

Lea Redmond

A PERIGEE BOOK

A PERIGEE BOOK
Published by the Penguin Group
Penguin Group (USA) LLC
375 Hudson Street, New York, New York 10014

USA • Canada • UK • Ireland • Australia • New Zealand • India • South Africa • China

penguin.com

A Penguin Random House Company

Library of Congress Cataloging-in-Publication Data

Redmond, Lea.
All lovely things : a field journal for the objects that define us / Lea Redmond.
pages cm
ISBN 978-0-399-17059-1 (paperback)
1. Scrapbook journaling. 2. Scrapbooks. 3. Handicraft—Miscellanea.   I. Title.
TT910.R79 2015
745.593'8—dc23   2014040066

First edition: March 2015

PRINTED IN THE UNITED STATES OF AMERICA

10   9   8   7   6   5   4   3   2   1

While the author has made every effort to provide accurate telephone numbers,
Internet addresses, and other contact information at the time of publication, neither the
publisher nor the author assumes any responsibility for errors, or for changes that occur
after publication. Further, the publisher does not have any control over and does not
assume any responsibility for author or third-party websites or their content.

Most Perigee books are available at special quantity discounts for bulk purchases
for sales promotions, premiums, fund-raising, or educational use. Special books,
or book excerpts, can also be created to fit specific needs. For details, write:
Special.Markets@us.penguingroup.com.

DEDICATED TO MY COLLEGE PROFESSORS:

Takemoto Sensei,
*who will always make time for
dancing with tea leaves.*

TKO,
*who teaches political theory with
action figures and coffee beans.*

Tom Davis,
*who showed me it is the spaces
in between things that matters most.*

LEA REDMOND
CALIFORNIA (CA)

YOU
HOME SWEET HOME

Dear You,

I am delighted that you have picked up this book. Nice to make your acquaintance! I poured my heart into it and I can't wait for us to get started. My name is Lea. I look sort of like this. Who are you?

I have something for you: this sea urchin shell. It has a story. I grew up on the Southern California coast and spent much of my childhood in the ocean, where I would snorkel with my father. He held my little hand as we floated through towers of kelp. When my father went scuba diving, he would return with small treasures for me. I remember the way his head would break the surface of the water, and how—speechlessly, before he pulled out his oxygen mouthpiece—he would hand me countless curiosities, such as this sea urchin shell. To me, these wordless gestures said: "Look at this wonder." "Isn't the world beautiful?" "Isn't this worth caring for?"

1

A human life on earth is unavoidably a richly material experience. Objects are everywhere! They are imbued with significance thanks to time, place, and circumstance. They influence who we are even when we're not paying attention to them. And the meaning of an object shifts from person to person.

In this field journal, you will explore humanity's relationship with objects by narrowing your focus to particular people and the definitive objects of their lives.

WHAT IS AN OBJECT?

We tend to think we know what an object is, so much so that it couldn't possibly need explaining. And yet, what truly is an object? How are our lives enriched when we pay special attention to material things? Grab a pencil and pull a favorite book off your bookshelf. Let's dig in.

Take a good, close look at your beloved book. Turn it over in your hands a bit. How old is it? How heavy? Check to see if there are dog-eared corners or notes in the margins. Quickly peek at a few pages inside. Try to remember your favorite parts, and think back to when you read it for the first time. How old were you? Where were you? Most importantly, who were you? The important thing about a beloved book, of course, is not the literal pages and ink, but the fact that you read it and loved it. It moved you and helped make you who you are today.

Now compare the significance of that favorite book to this one—this brand-new book that you have only just begun. Pick up this one for a minute and notice its crisp edges and clean pages. It feels like the difference between a dear old friend and someone you've only just met, doesn't it? In time—as you fill these pages—this book will become heavy with significance too. It will transform right in front of your eyes, from an unfamiliar lump of paper into a unique, one-of-a-kind treasure.

This magic trick called "meaning" is not just for books, of course. It holds true for all objects—shoes, seashells, a teapot, a watermelon. All things—from the mundane to the marvelous—have the potential to gather meaning of various qualities and quantities. Objects have diverse roles: practical tools, memory sparks, status symbols, historical record keeping, fine art. They're fascinating companions in the world that invite us to explore, learn, work, connect, and develop a unique sense of self. A close look at the formative objects of our lives can say a lot about who we are, who we once were, and who we are becoming. It can even give us a sneak peek into who—deep down—we most wish to be.

Let's practice. In the next few pages, I'll guide you through a series of "object experiments" designed to enrich our notion of "objects." Doing these little exercises will likely expand the quantity—and enrich the quality—of the objects we draw into our journals. While the first thing that comes to mind when we think about people's objects might be their personal possessions, in the pages ahead, you'll practice widening your scope and seeing much more.

Look around your home and choose three objects that are important to you. For the purposes of this book, an "object" is any phenomenon that has obvious physical form. These are tangible items that you can see, hear, taste, smell, or touch. As you identify your three objects, observe the thoughts, emotions, and memories they call to mind. Take time to notice a detail about each, and then draw them here:

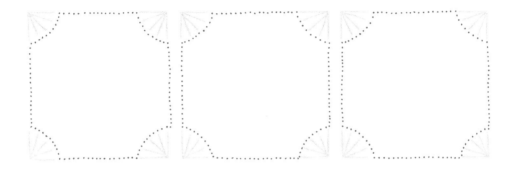

I'm guessing that your three objects make perfect sense to you. They are familiar and it is probably fairly clear to you why you chose them. After you've filled the three boxes above, take a moment to consider the following three objects that are important to me: watercolor paints, chess pieces, and a big beetle.

Compared to your three objects, mine appear a bit mysterious, no? They are recognizable to you—you can indeed identify what they are—but you can only guess at why exactly they are important to *me*.

It turns out that the meaning of objects doesn't belong entirely to the objects themselves, tucked tidily within their physical edges. It also belongs to us. Sure, lots of people might agree that a chocolate cake is almost always a happy sight, but at the same time, the meaning of things is far from pinned down. For one person, a cake holds a memory of a sixteenth birthday, while for another, it recalls the time a dog jumped up at the kitchen counter and indulged in a big treat!

One special gift of objects is that they help carry—and cause—*stories*. Working in this journal will likely spark memories, explanations, mysteries, and musings. There is a story archive toward the back of this book for moments when you want to record the story that accompanies an object. You can flip to page 194 and take a peek. There you will find the story of my watercolor paints, Emily Dickinson's picnic basket, and a few other things. (When I add a note to the archive, I like to add a little star next to the object, just to mark the fact that there is a story in the archive that goes with it.)

OBJECT EXPERIMENT 2: Made by Nature

The objects that easily come to mind are oftentimes the ones made by human beings—true artifacts—but there is plenty of room here for nature's creations too—for a beech leaf, a bumblebee, fossils. Besides, the line dividing "human-made" and "nature-made" in our minds is actually a bit of a fiction. Who or what is truly responsible for the existence of a willow basket full of wild blueberries? Feel free to include natural objects in your character vignettes when they are relevant for a person's life story.

In the box below, draw a natural object that is meaningful to you. It might be in your home, or it might remain in its natural home where you experienced it, such as a hummingbird in a friend's backyard or some wildflowers on a hike.

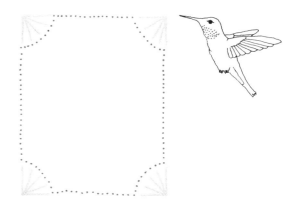

OBJECT EXPERIMENT 3: All Five Senses

Not all "things" are visible. In addition to objects that we can easily see, there are scents, sounds, tastes, and even textures. Remember to include some of these more elusive objects. For example, maybe you live above a bakery and the scent of bread out your window is wonderfully comforting; you might not ever eat the bread, but draw a loaf anyway since you love the scent.

SOUND OF A CHURCH BELL   HUMIDITY   GRAPEFRUIT'S FLAVOR   SCENT OF BREAD BAKING

Let's practice translating the less graspable phenomena of sensory experience into visual form. In the box, draw something to communicate an important scent, sound, taste, or texture.

A full moon and the *Mona Lisa* share something—both objects are out of reach. The moon—at 238,900 miles away—is literally out of reach. The *Mona Lisa* painting is simply not for the taking. For this book, ownership is not required. If you have encountered an object in the world and it spoke to your soul, it is *yours* in the only way that truly matters. Sad but true, I will never own a USS *Enterprise* spaceship. But I drew it in my journal because watching *The Next Generation* with my dad in middle school gave me hope that there was more to life than teenage schoolyard drama.

Let's give this a try. Draw a significant object for each box.

own   do not own   cannot own

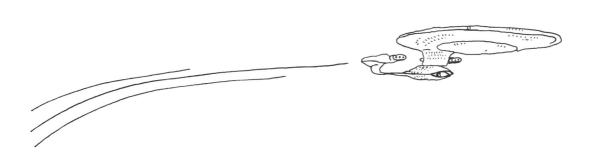

It is tempting to fill this book with favorite things—the items we find most pleasing or that make us happy, like the piano music that Charles Darwin found soothing. I hope your portraits include many pleasant items, but I also invite you to include some serious things. A fulfilling and true vignette can include a full range of emotional experience.

A single object might even carry both joy and grief. In the vignette I drew of my grandfather, I included a dance card that he found taped into my grandmother's diary after she passed away. The half-heart card—from 1941—is surrounded by my grandmother's handwritten notes about her fondness for my grandfather.

Give it a try. Draw items in response to the emotions listed in the boxes below. The items can be autobiographical or belong to someone else.

peaceful

nostalgic

hope

One thing you might notice as you pay special attention to objects is both the joy and the burden of things' tangibility. Objects can be lovely to look at and hold, but they can also pile up! Our attachment to things is both beautiful and difficult. There is sadness in a hand-knit sweater full of moth holes or a pile of old love letters. To become the people we most want to be, sometimes we need to let go of things. At the same time, there is hope and optimism in the making of a new object. Sometimes we need to add new things to our lives: a new tool, a special gift, a bicycle, a baby stroller. In the boxes below, draw one thing you would like to let go of and one thing you would like to acquire.

let go

acquire

Only a couple of sea urchin shells from my childhood collection remain. And one of them recently broke into too many pieces to count. My heart sank! It immediately sparked memories of seaweed and salt spray and my father, whom I adore. And here is a very important point: Things come and go. My shell can be damaged or lost. But the story lives on inside me because that shell has helped make me who I am.

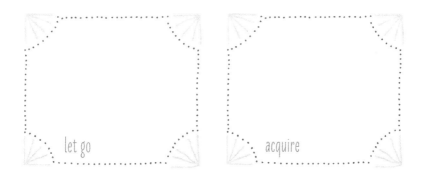

ONTO THE PAGE AND INTO THE FIELD

In the pages ahead, you'll find a whole heap of empty portrait pages waiting for you. You can feature whoever is important to you: famous folks you admire, fictional characters from novels, and loved ones—real people you know personally like friends and family members—even yourself! If you already have a few ideas for people to include, jot them down here:

....

....

....

THESE ARE SOME OF THE FOLKS THAT ARE IMPORTANT TO ME.

MY MOM   MY FRIEND DAVE   MY PAST SELF   MY GRANDFATHER

EMILY DICKINSON   GANDHI   CHARLES DARWIN   HENRY DAVID THOREAU

ALICE   BASHO   CHARLES AND RAY EAMES

On page 190, you will find advice on how to determine the objects of people's lives. You can also interview your subjects if they are loved ones, or loan the journal to friends to be "guest" portraitists. On page 191, you'll find a list of interview questions that can help you uncover good objects stories. (You can see what my friend Dave drew when I loaned him my journal.)

In the portrait pages, you'll also see that many of the compartments contain words. These prompts are to jog your memory, spark ideas, and guide your search for significant objects. Some of these prompts are fairly straightforward while others lend themselves to creative interpretation. These words are meant to be inspiring, not constraining. You may take them or leave them as you see fit! Here are a few ways to work with them:

* Respond literally, using it like a category
* Respond metaphorically or by creative association
* Cross it out and replace with a new word from the list on page 192
* If the box is prompt-less, add your own
* Leave the box without any words and let the objects speak for themselves

You are welcome to fill in the portrait pages using whatever medium and technique you prefer. Choose one approach for the entire book, or mix it up!

Here are some examples:

GRANDMOTHER'S
SALT SHAKER
GLASS, 1940s

A tip: I recommend drawing the objects in pencil first, just to get the main shapes right before setting them with ink or color. Another tip: draw with real-life example objects in front of you, or while referring to photographs you've taken on your phone, or from images you've found online. You can even print these out and trace them.

I hope you are not intimidated to bring your pen to these pages. Skilled renderings can certainly be lovely, but for this book they are really secondary—perhaps even largely beside the point. The joyful task here is selecting objects and reflecting upon them. The goal isn't prettiness, but meaning. If you can make a muffin, you can draw in this book. Filling in the compartments should be as easy and lighthearted as dropping batter into a muffin pan. Just go for it and do your best.

THE PORTRAITIST'S EYE

Portraits don't paint themselves. Behind every portrait is a *portraitist* who tries to portray the essence, likeness, interests, even moods of her subject. Even more important, a portraitist has a perspective—his or her own unique way of looking at her subject as well as at the larger world. A person's true, complete identity can never be pinned down in tidy rows like Darwin's beetle collection. But the pleasure of this book is trying to nevertheless and enjoying the thoughts and conversations that surface along the way.*

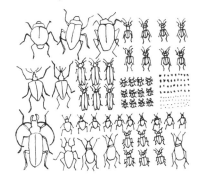

----

* Please note that even though the characters portrayed in this book are real people, the objects of their lives have been creatively interpreted. The facts are true to the best of my knowledge, and when it was not clear exactly what a particular historical artifact looked like, I did some research, chose something of the era, and made my best guess.

LOVELY YOU

This book is a bit of a matryoshka—a Russian nesting doll. In the center are the meanings—both evident and latent—carried by the objects you add to the book. The second layer is the objects themselves, in all their tangible glory. The next level out is the collection of people you choose to portray—the people that are defined by the objects. And the final layer is you because you get to choose the people and how they are portrayed. Considered together, everything inside this book inevitably paints a picture of *you*.

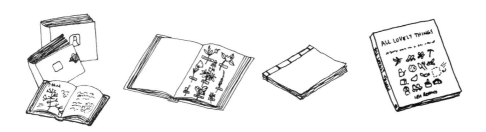

A field journal, at its best, is not a mere record of reality—of what already is. It is not a straightforward transfer of the world onto the page. Rather, it is for seeing things in new ways and honing one's attention. This journal can reveal patterns, enrich our relationships, and maybe even inspire us to become more us—more human, more me, more you. This book has the potential to become a meaningful object. It is just waiting for you to bring it to life.

I will sign off in the way I have done for years . . .

All lovely things,
Lea Redmond

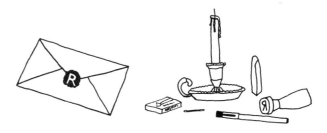

portrait

notes

name

important

often

freedom

family

hand-me-down

leisure

passion

type of plant

wonder

adventure

treat

favorite

toy

gift

portrait

notes

name

beautiful

adventure

inspiration

hobby

metaphor

childhood

love

curiosity

friendship

tradition

portrait

name

notes

adventure

heirloom

passion

childhood

small

precious

play

big

tool

surprise

care

often

daily

pleasure

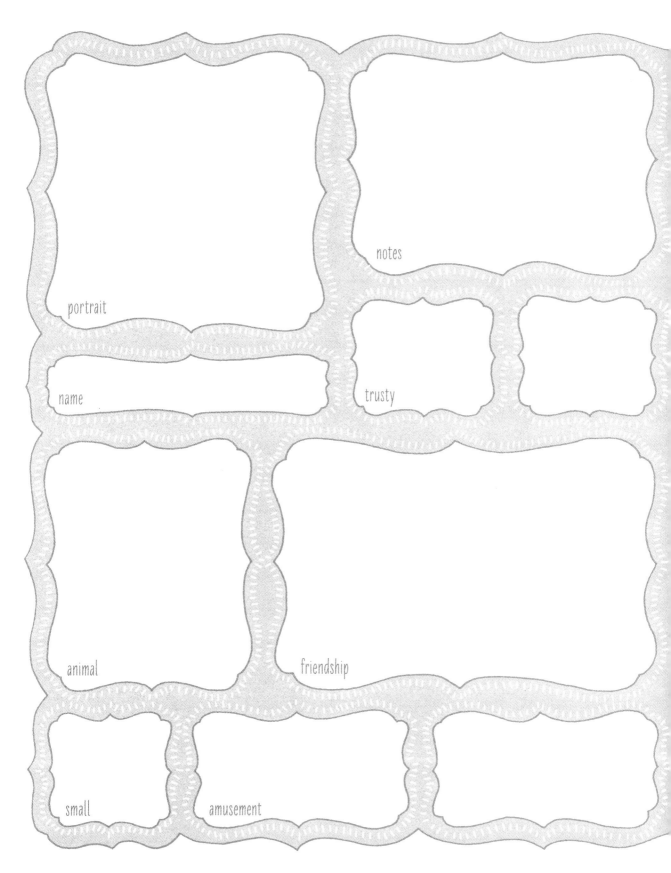

portrait

notes

name

trusty

animal

friendship

small

amusement

treat

surprise

antique

type of plant

clothing / shoes

tool

portrait

notes

name

for hours and hours

love

gift

adventure

accomplishment

family

hobby

small

childhood

playful

old

mystery

big

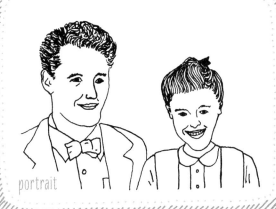
portrait

CHARLES AND RAY EAMES TOOK PLAY SERIOUSLY AND DELIGHTED IN EVERYDAY OBJECTS. A PARABLE HIDES IN A BANANA LEAF. A HONEYMOON LINGERS IN A PIECE OF TUMBLEWEED. "EVERYTHING EVENTUALLY CONNECTS— PEOPLE, IDEAS, OBJECTS." —C.E.

notes

CHARLES & RAY EAMES

name

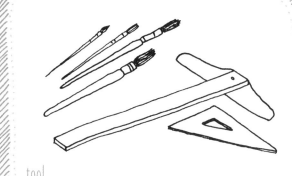
tool

love

tradition

collection

play

daily

antique

pleasure

serious

trusty

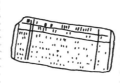

delight

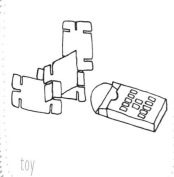

toy

inspiration

portrait

notes

name

childhood

for hours and hours

companion

hobby

accomplished

home

gift

playful

delight

inspiration

portrait

name

notes

freedom

gift

passion

handmade

dream

mass-produced

hope

romance

love

family

relaxation

lots and lots

nostalgic

portrait

notes

name

trusty

reminder

vehicle

daily

often

freedom

companion

handmade

essential

tool

portrait

notes

name

romantic

philosophical

mentor

from a book

for hours and hours

antique

metaphor

heirloom

nature

often

lovely

inspiration

reminder

ponder

portrait

notes

name

leisure

curiosity

new

winter

a great idea

favorite book

courage

childhood

family

delicious

kindness

someday

portrait

notes

name

childhood

summer

passion

courage

home

companion

pleasure

for hours and hours

tradition

type of plant

portrait

I LOVE THE THOUGHT OF A CHILDHOOD HOBBY — BEETLE COLLECTING — EVENTUALLY LEADING TO SOMETHING AS IMPORTANT AS THE THEORY OF EVOLUTION. EVERYTHING ALWAYS STARTS SOMEWHERE, EH?

notes

CHARLES DARWIN

name

adventure

heirloom

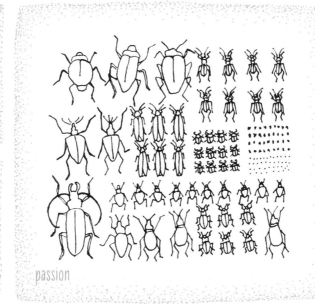

passion

childhood

small

precious

play

big

tool

surprise

care

often

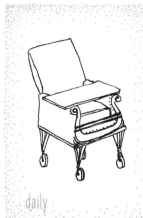

daily

pleasure

portrait

notes

name

treasured

mystery

good memories

friend

love

work

wish

summer

ritual

portrait

notes

name

identity

home

tool

poetic

vehicle

old

nature

sound

food / beverage

play

clothing / shoes

ritual

borrowed

surprise

childhood

portrait

name

love

notes

tool

tradition

collection

play

daily

antique

pleasure

serious

trusty

delight

toy

inspiration

portrait

notes

name

beautiful

adventure

inspiration

hobby

metaphor

childhood

love

curiosity

friendship

tradition

portrait

notes

name

food / beverage

beautiful

solitary

collection

nature

friendship

inspiration

home

furniture

tool

community

travel

essential

family

metaphor

portrait

OH, HOW I WOULD LOVE TO STUMBLE UPON THE RABBIT HOLE THAT YOUNG ALICE DID! THE BEST I CAN DO IS KEEP AN EYE OUT FOR THE MAGIC, PLAYFULNESS, AND ABSURDITY THAT REAL LIFE OFFERS...

notes

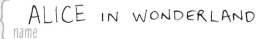

ALICE IN WONDERLAND

name

trusty

Drink me

animal

friendship

small

amusement

treat

surprise

antique

type of plant

clothing / shoes

tool

portrait

notes

name

for hours and hours

love

gift

adventure

accomplishment

family

hobby

small

childhood

playful

old

mystery

big

portrait

notes

name

important

often

freedom

hand-me-down

family

leisure

passion

type of plant

wonder

adventure

treat

favorite

toy

gift

portrait

notes

name

childhood

for hours and hours

companion

hobby

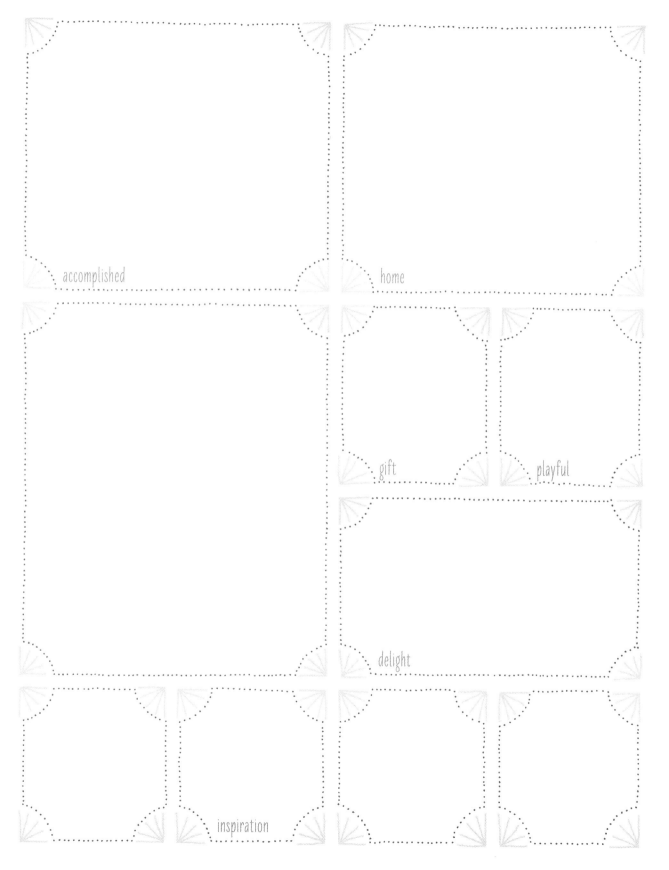

accomplished

home

gift

playful

delight

inspiration

portrait

name

notes

adventure

heirloom

passion

childhood

small

precious

play

big

tool

surprise

care

often

daily

pleasure

portrait

notes

name

trusty

animal

friendship

small

amusement

treat

surprise

antique

type of plant

clothing / shoes

tool

BASHO DRIFTED LIKE A LONE
CLOUD THROUGH THE JAPANESE
COUNTRYSIDE, TRAVELING BY FOOT
AND WRITING POEMS ALONG THE WAY
UNDER THE MOON. HE WROTE IN
HIS JOURNAL:

"THE JOURNEY ITSELF IS HOME."

BASHŌ

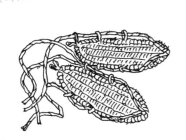

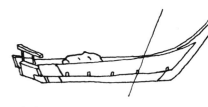

old

nature

sound

play

food / beverage

ritual

clothing / shoes

borrowed

surprise

childhood

portrait

name

leisure

winter

a great idea

notes

curiosity

new

favorite book

courage

childhood

family

delicious

kindness

someday

portrait

notes

name

childhood

summer

passion

courage

home

companion

tradition

pleasure

for hours and hours

type of plant

portrait

notes

name

freedom

gift

passion

handmade

dream

mass-produced

romance

love

hope

family

relaxation

lots and lots

nostalgic

portrait

notes

name

trusty

reminder

vehicle

daily

often

freedom

companion

handmade

essential

tool

portrait

notes

name

romantic

philosophical

mentor

from a book

for hours and hours

antique

metaphor

heirloom

nature

often

lovely

inspiration

reminder

ponder

portrait

name

notes

tool

love

collection

tradition

play

daily

antique

pleasure

serious

trusty

delight

toy

inspiration

portrait

EMILY REMINDS ME THAT IT IS OKAY TO BE ALONE. SOMETIMES SOLITUDE IS NECESSARY TO HEAR ONESELF THINK AND TO MAKE BEAUTIFUL THINGS. AND I LOVE THAT SHE ATTACHED POEMS TO HOMEMADE CANDIES AND FLOWER BOUQUETS!

notes

EMILY DICKINSON
name

childhood

for hours and hours

companion

hobby

accomplished

home

gift

playful

delight

inspiration

portrait

notes

name

food / beverage

beautiful

solitary

collection

nature

friendship

inspiration

home

furniture

tool

community

travel

essential

family

metaphor

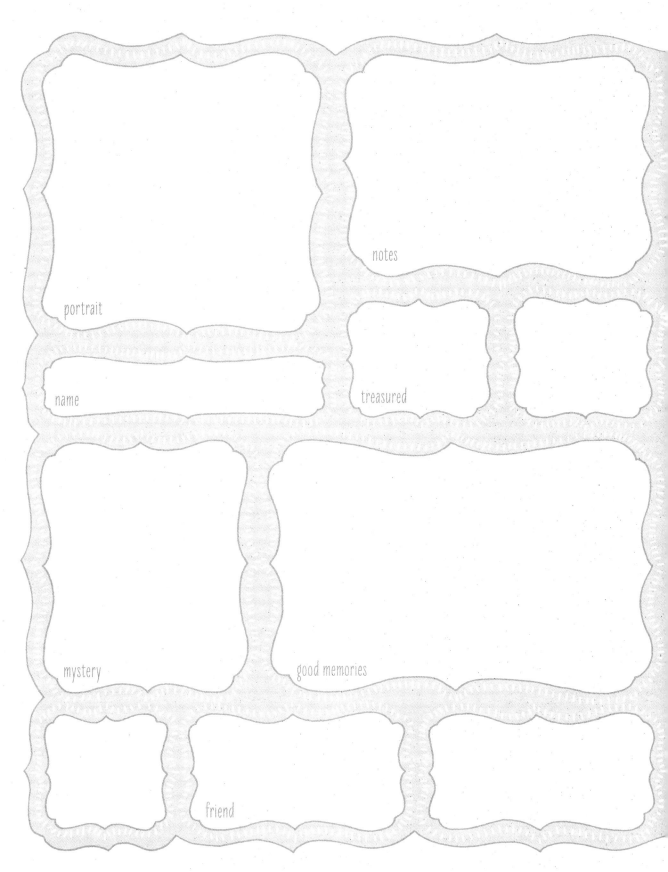

portrait

notes

name

treasured

mystery

good memories

friend

love

work

wish

summer

ritual

portrait

notes

name

identity

home

tool

poetic

vehicle

old

nature

sound

play

food / beverage

clothing / shoes

ritual

borrowed

surprise

childhood

portrait

notes

name

important

often

freedom

family

hand-me-down

leisure

passion

type of plant

wonder

adventure

treat

favorite

toy

gift

portrait

notes

name

beautiful

adventure

inspiration

hobby

metaphor

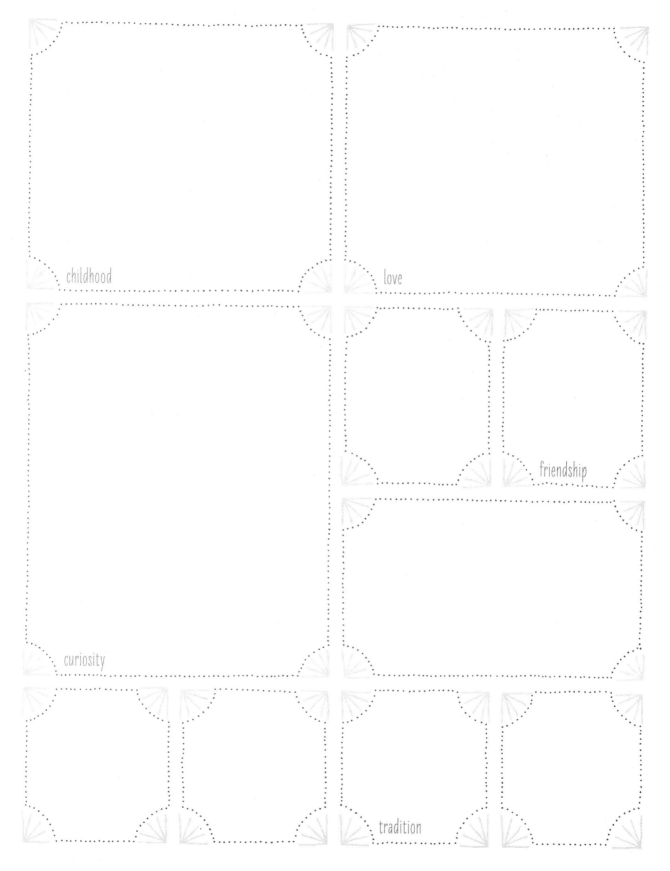

childhood

love

friendship

curiosity

tradition

portrait

name

notes

adventure

heirloom

passion

childhood

small

precious

play

big

tool

surprise

care

often

daily

pleasure

portrait

notes

name

trusty

animal

friendship

small

amusement

treat

surprise

antique

type of plant

clothing / shoes

tool

portrait

I AM ALWAYS LOOKING FOR THE POEM HIDING INSIDE THINGS. I KEEP AN EYE OUT FOR THE MOMENTS WHEN THE ORDINARY SLIPS INTO THE EXTRAORDINARY.

notes

THE AUTHOR

name

romantic

philosophical

mentor

from a book

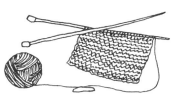

for hours and hours

antique

metaphor

heirloom

nature

often

lovely

inspiration

ponder

reminder

portrait

notes

name

leisure

curiosity

new

winter

a great idea

favorite book

courage

childhood

family

delicious

kindness

someday

portrait

notes

name

childhood

for hours and hours

companion

hobby

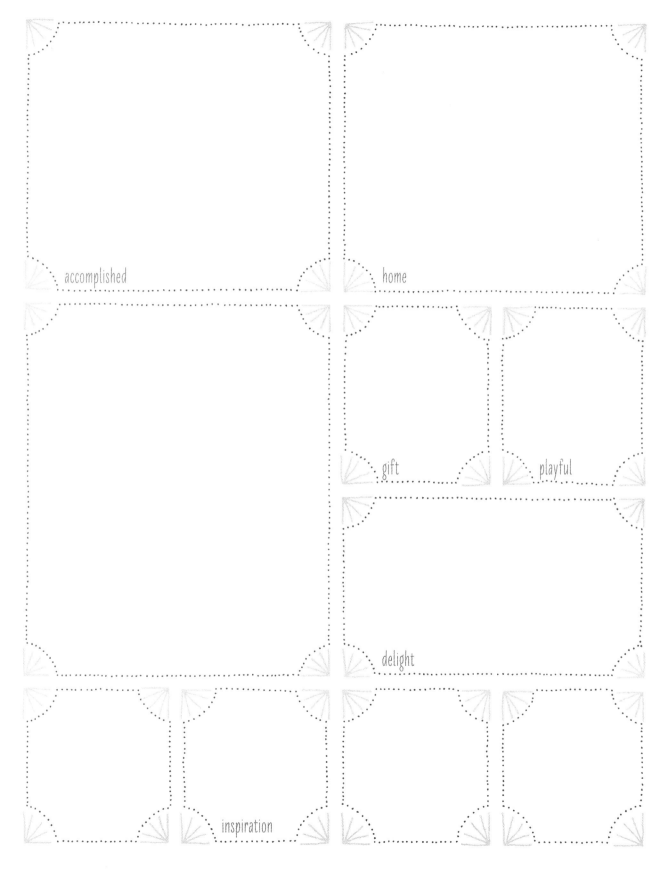

accomplished

home

gift

playful

delight

inspiration

portrait

name

notes

freedom

gift

passion

handmade

dream

mass-produced

romance

love

hope

family

relaxation

lots and lots

nostalgic

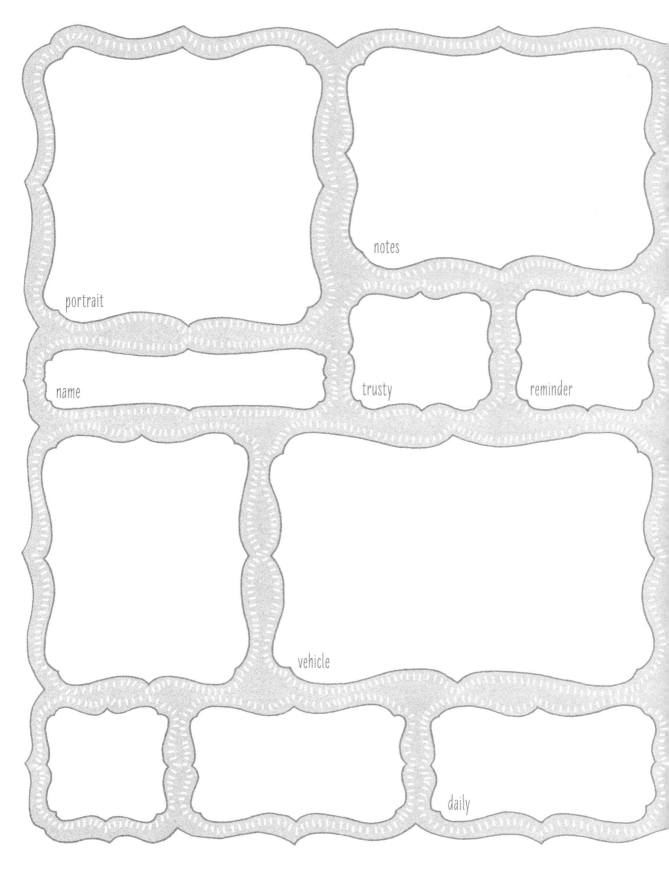

portrait

notes

name

trusty

reminder

vehicle

daily

often

freedom

companion

handmade

essential

tool

portrait

notes

name

for hours and hours

love

gift

adventure

accomplishment

family

hobby

small

childhood

playful

old

mystery

big

portrait

AS A CHILD, I MADE THINGS CONSTANTLY. GIVE ME SOME ORIGAMI PAPER AND I WAS HAPPILY ENGAGED FOR HOURS. I HAVE ALWAYS LOVED SMALL OBJECTS — THE ONES MADE BY PEOPLE AS WELL AS THE ONES MADE BY NATURE.

notes

THE AUTHOR (AS A CHILD)

name

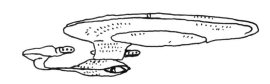
important

often

freedom

hand-me-down

family

family

leisure

leisure

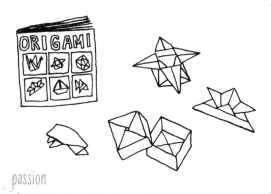
passion

type of plant

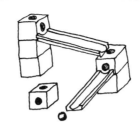

wonder

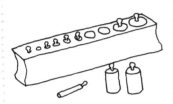

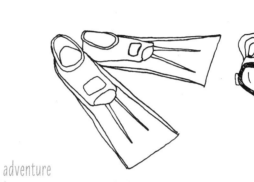

adventure

treat

favorite

toy

gift

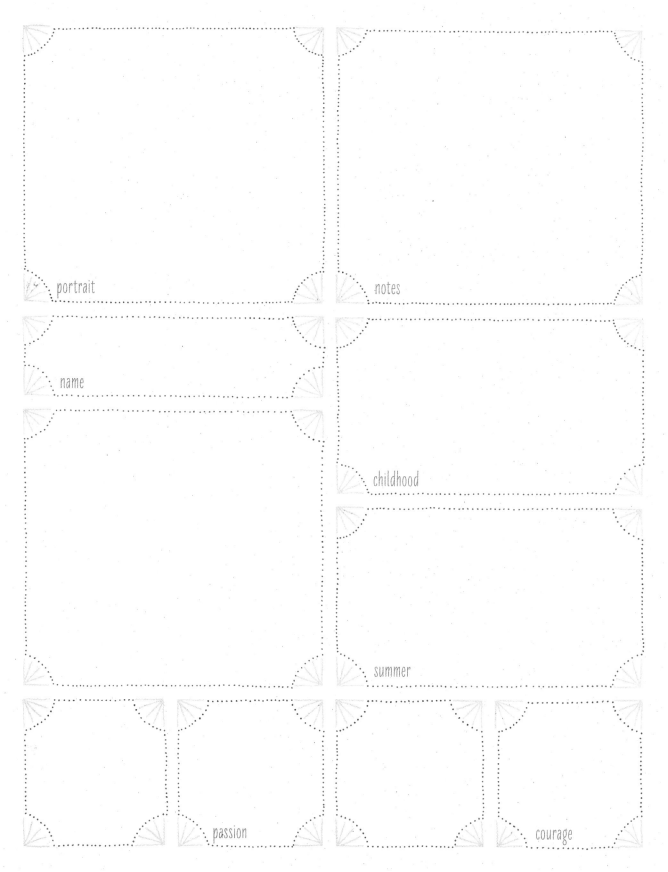

portrait

notes

name

childhood

summer

passion

courage

home

pleasure

companion

for hours and hours

tradition

type of plant

portrait

notes

name

food / beverage

beautiful

solitary

collection

nature

friendship

inspiration

home

furniture

tool

community

travel

essential

family

metaphor

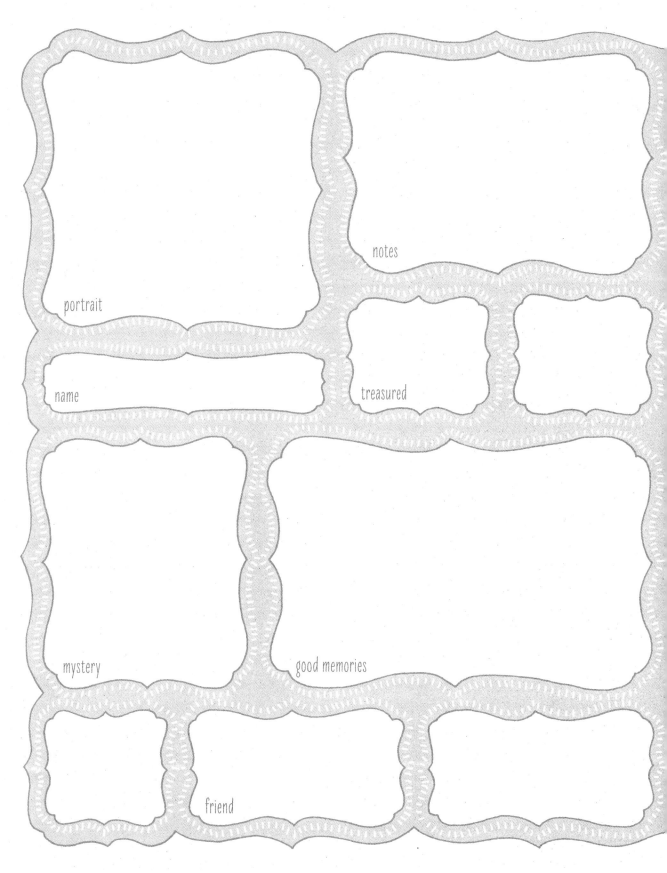

portrait

notes

name

treasured

mystery

good memories

friend

love

work

wish

summer

ritual

portrait

notes

name

romantic

philosophical

mentor

from a book

for hours and hours

antique

metaphor

heirloom

nature

often

inspiration

lovely

reminder

ponder

portrait

notes

name

love

tool

tradition

collection

play

daily

antique

pleasure

serious

trusty

delight

toy

inspiration

portrait

Hi Lea
Looking back,
Looking forward-
So many sparkling
times to share!
Love, mom

notes

Lea Ann
my daughter
name

beautiful

adventure

inspiration

hobby

metaphor

childhood

love

curiosity

img_group

friendship

tradition

portrait

name

notes

adventure

heirloom

passion

childhood

small

precious

play

big

tool

surprise

care

often

daily

pleasure

portrait

notes

name

trusty

animal

friendship

small

amusement

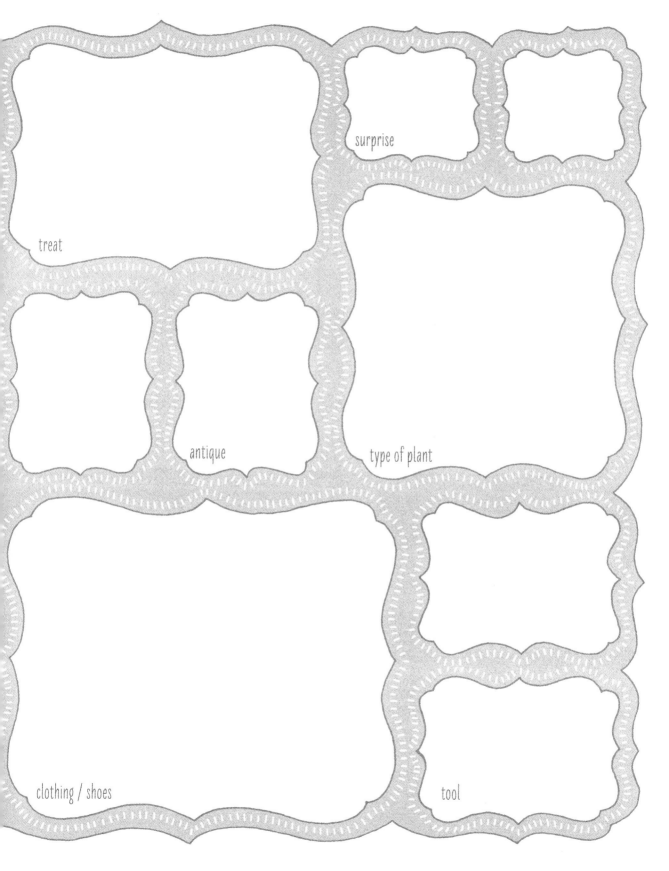

treat

surprise

antique

type of plant

clothing / shoes

tool

portrait

notes

name

identity

home

tool

poetic

vehicle

old

nature

sound

play

food / beverage

clothing / shoes

ritual

borrowed

surprise

childhood

portrait

notes

name

important

often

freedom

hand-me-down

family

leisure

passion

type of plant

wonder

adventure

treat

favorite

toy

gift

portrait

MY GRANDFATHER IS A TOTAL
SWEETHEART. HE IS FULL
OF STORIES AND FULL OF
LIFE. WATCHING HIM AND MY
GRANDMOTHER OVER THE YEARS,
I LEARNED WHAT LOVE LOOKS
LIKE.

notes

GRANDFATHER JIM
name

childhood

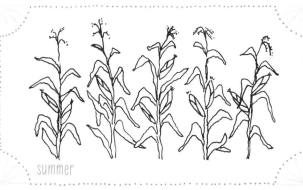
summer

passion

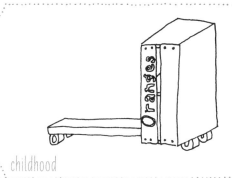

courage

home

companion

pleasure

for hours and hours

tradition

type of plant

portrait

notes

name

freedom

gift

passion

handmade

dream

mass-produced

hope

romance

love

family

relaxation

lots and lots

nostalgic

portrait

notes

name

trusty

reminder

vehicle

daily

often

freedom

companion

handmade

essential

tool

portrait

notes

name

for hours and hours

love

gift

adventure

accomplishment

family

hobby

small

childhood

playful

old

mystery

big

portrait

notes

name

leisure

winter

curiosity

new

a great idea

favorite book

courage

childhood

family

delicious

kindness

someday

portrait

notes

name

beautiful

adventure

inspiration

hobby

metaphor

childhood

love

friendship

curiosity

tradition

portrait

MY MOM IS ONE OF MY BEST
FRIENDS. SHE IS CHEERFUL,
INFINITELY SUPPORTIVE, AND
BURSTING WITH CREATIVE IDEAS
AND INSIGHTS. WE CAN TALK
UP A STORM TOGETHER!

notes

name

GINGER,
THE AUTHOR'S MOM

freedom

gift

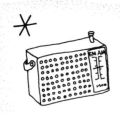

LOVE ME DO

Capitol Records   72076

THE BEATLES

passion

handmade

dream

mass-produced

hope

romance

love

family

relaxation

lots and lots

nostalgic

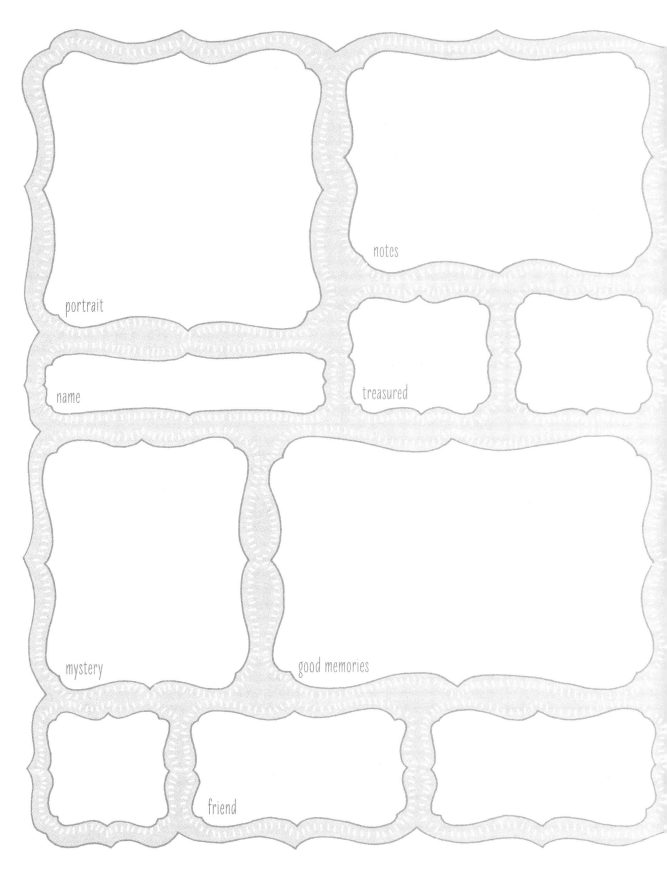

portrait

notes

name

treasured

mystery

good memories

friend

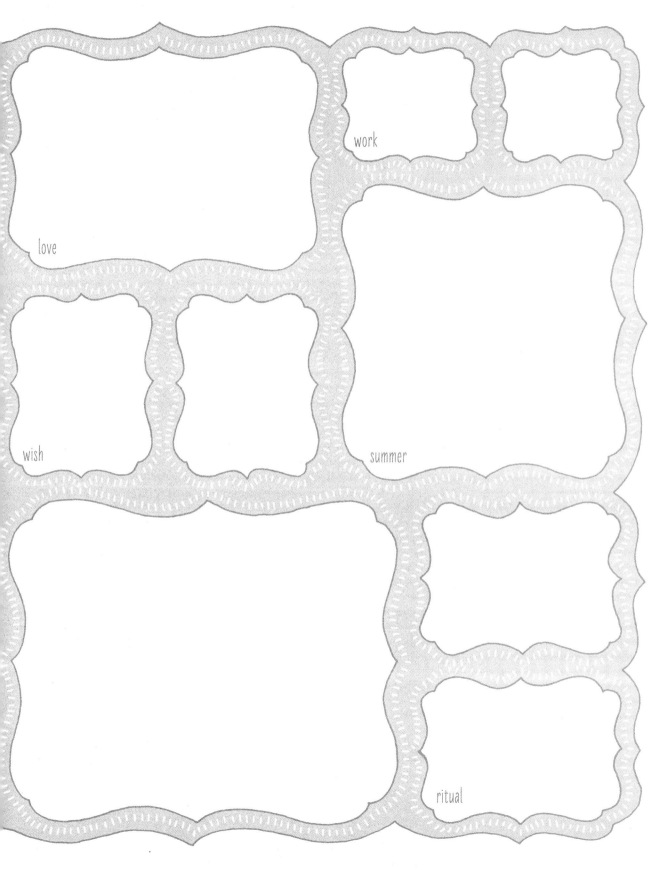

love

work

wish

summer

ritual

portrait

notes

name

romantic

philosophical

mentor

from a book

for hours and hours

antique

metaphor

heirloom

nature

often

inspiration

lovely

reminder

ponder

portrait

name

love

collection

play

notes

tool

tradition

daily

antique

pleasure

serious

trusty

delight

toy

inspiration

portrait

notes

name

childhood

for hours and hours

companion

hobby

accomplished

home

gift

playful

delight

inspiration

portrait

name

notes

food / beverage

beautiful

solitary

collection

nature

friendship

inspiration

home

furniture

tool

essential

community

travel

family

metaphor

portrait

notes

MAHATMA GANDHI
name

trusty

reminder

vehicle

daily

often

freedom

companion

essential

handmade

tool

portrait

notes

name

identity

home

tool

poetic

vehicle

old

nature

sound

food / beverage

play

clothing / shoes

ritual

borrowed

surprise

childhood

portrait

notes

name

often

freedom

important

family

hand-me-down

leisure

passion

type of plant

wonder

adventure

treat

favorite

toy

gift

portrait

notes

name

childhood

summer

passion

courage

home

pleasure

companion

for hours and hours

tradition

type of plant

portrait

name

notes

adventure

heirloom

passion

childhood

small

precious

play

big

tool

surprise

care

often

daily

pleasure

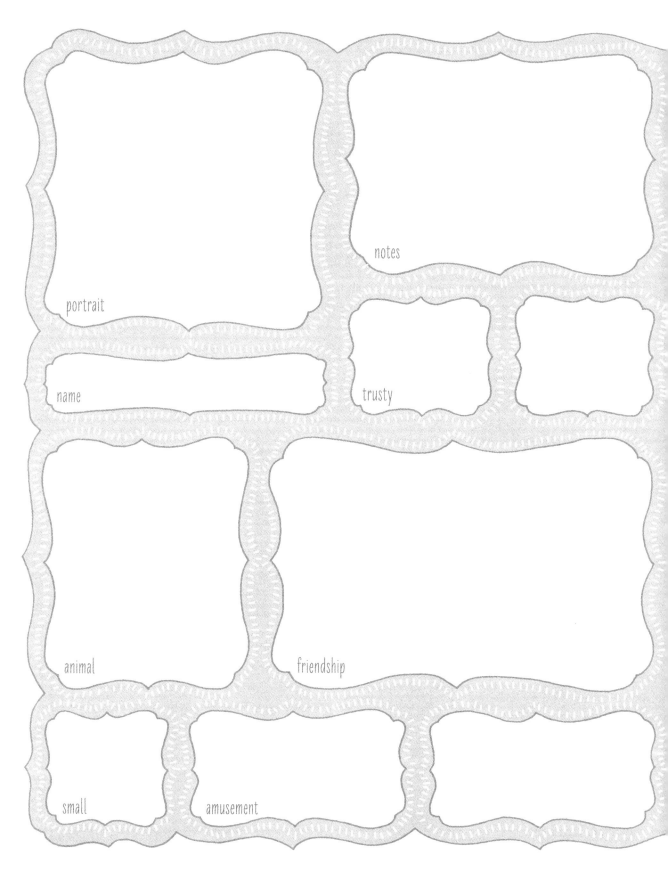

portrait

notes

name

trusty

animal

friendship

small

amusement

treat

surprise

antique

type of plant

clothing / shoes

tool

portrait

notes

name

for hours and hours

love

gift

adventure

accomplishment

family

hobby

small

childhood

playful

old

mystery

big

portrait

I'm Lea's friend from the East Coast. I like to learn how things work and I'd like to know each thing's name.

notes

name

Dave Unger

important

often

Northampton
Public Library

1842 Dave Unger

freedom

hand-me-down

family

passion

leisure

type of plant

wonder

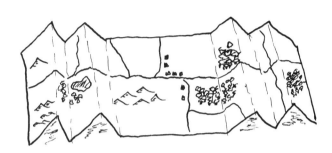

adventure

treat

favorite

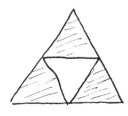

toy

gift

portrait

notes

name

beautiful

adventure

inspiration

hobby

metaphor

childhood

love

curiosity

friendship

tradition

portrait

name

notes

freedom

gift

passion

handmade

dream

mass-produced

romance

love

hope

family

relaxation

lots and lots

nostalgic

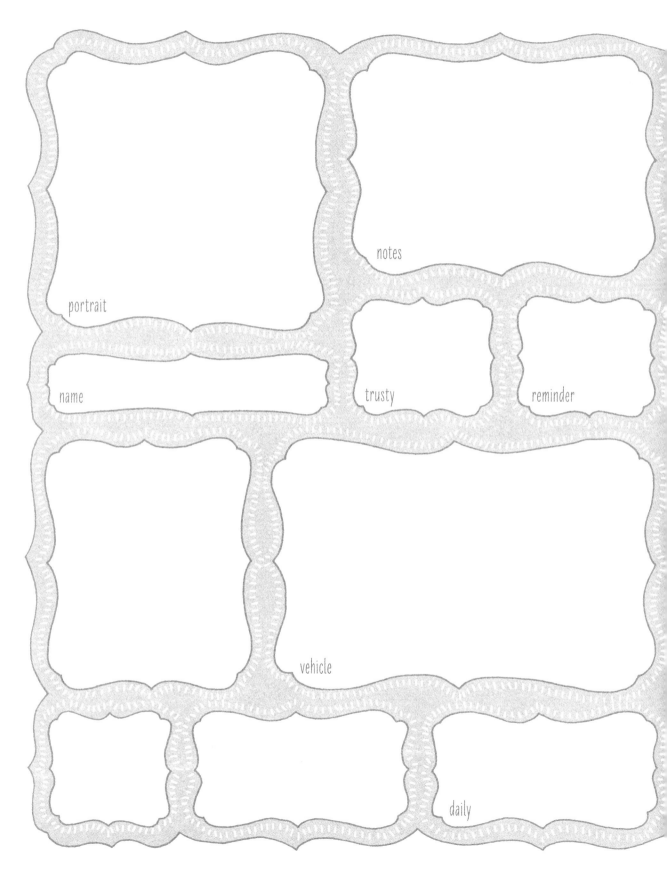

portrait

notes

name

trusty

reminder

vehicle

daily

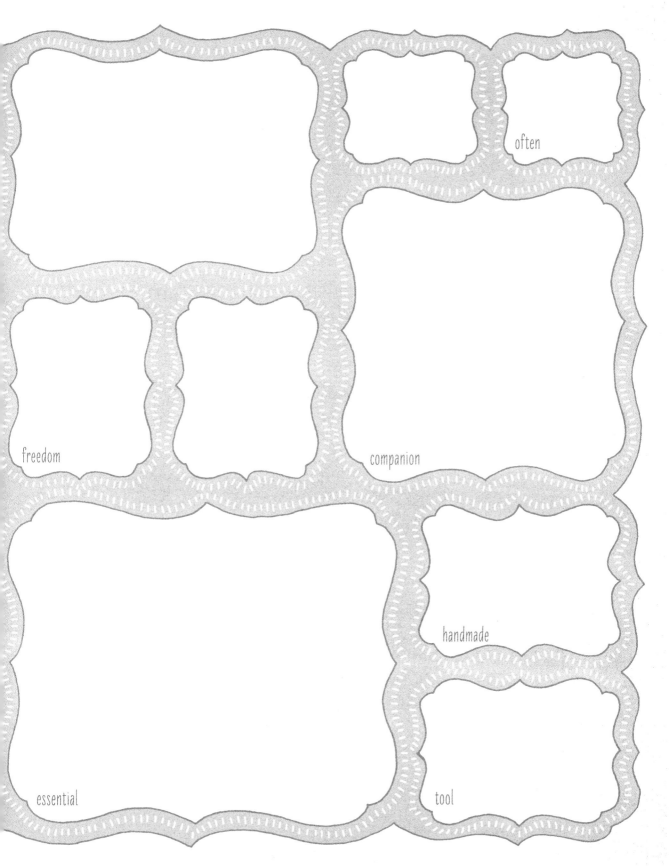

often

freedom

companion

handmade

essential

tool

portrait

notes

name

romantic

philosophical

mentor

from a book

for hours and hours

antique

metaphor

heirloom

nature

often

lovely

inspiration

reminder

ponder

portrait

name

notes

leisure

curiosity

new

winter

a great idea

favorite book

courage

childhood

family

delicious

kindness

someday

portrait

notes

name

childhood

for hours and hours

companion

hobby

accomplished

home

gift

playful

delight

inspiration

portrait

FROM THOREAU, I LEARNED THE IMPORTANCE OF STARTING FROM SCRATCH. QUESTION EVERYTHING. BE THOUGHTFUL. SEE THROUGH THE SURFACE TO THE ESSENCE. SEEK YOUR TRUEST SELF.

notes

HENRY DAVID THOREAU

name

food / beverage

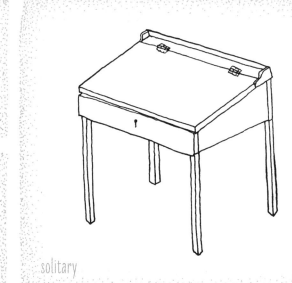
solitary

beautiful

nature

collection

friendship

inspiration

home

furniture

tool

community

travel

essential

family

metaphor

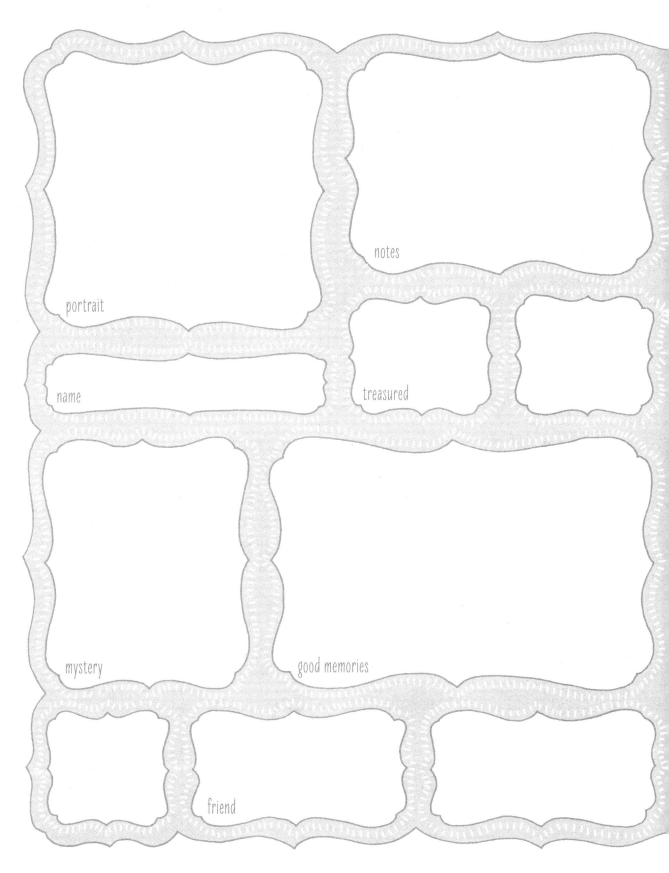

portrait

name

notes

treasured

mystery

good memories

friend

love

work

wish

summer

ritual

portrait

notes

name

identity

home

tool

poetic

vehicle

old

nature

sound

play

food / beverage

ritual

clothing / shoes

borrowed

surprise

childhood

portrait

notes

name

love

tool

tradition

collection

play

daily

antique

pleasure

serious

trusty

delight

toy

inspiration

portrait

notes

name

childhood

summer

passion

courage

home

pleasure

companion

for hours and hours

tradition

type of plant

portrait

notes

name

food / beverage

beautiful

solitary

collection

nature

friendship

inspiration

home

furniture

tool

community

travel

essential

family

metaphor

QUITE A CHARACTER: CHOOSING YOUR SUBJECTS

When deciding who to feature in this journal, you can draw people you know personally, public figures you admire, folks you're curious about from afar, or even people who exist purely in your imagination. Here are some sparks to get you thinking:

* A favorite author, artist, actor, musician, scientist, politician, chef
* A fictional character from a novel, play, movie, TV show
* Someone you've always wanted to know more about
* Autobiographical vignettes of yourself at various ages
* Family members
* Friends and romantic interests, past and present
* A hypothetical person from an ancient (or future) culture
* Imaginary characters that you dream up

DO YOUR HOMEWORK (OR LET THE DOG EAT IT)

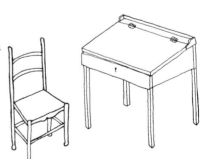

There are many ways to identify the significant objects of a person's life. Whether your subject is an admired historical figure, a loved one, or a past version of yourself, you can use the following approaches:

* Read a biography or conduct research online
* Watch a film (documentary or historical fiction)
* Read a novel or watch a movie or TV serial drama
* Look at paintings in a museum
* Invent a fictional character
* Take a trip down memory lane and reminisce
* Invent the future you that you would like to be
* Interview someone (in person or over the phone)
* Loan your book to a loved one for them to draw their own page

It's much easier to create a list of wonderful objects than you might think. Many methods work well, and it's largely a matter of personal style. If you don't want to read a 600-page biography, just read an online biography! I did my Gandhi vignette almost entirely from quick online research and watching the movie *Gandhi*. With whatever approach you use, pay special attention to the objects mentioned or shown. Sometimes they are hidden in the shadows. I like to use sticky notes in books. I pause movies and snap photos of the screen with my phone. And, by all means, if research feels tedious, just make your best guess and proceed!

STEP INTO A REPORTER'S SHOES

Guide people to remember and share the important objects of their lives using the following interview questions. Add your own! Before beginning an interview, choose which page of prompts you will use.

* Does the word .... (insert **prompt** from journal compartment) bring any objects to mind for you? What objects in your life remind you of .... (insert prompt)?
* **List** any 10 objects that are important to you. Tell me the stories that make them meaningful.
* What are some of the most important **moments** of your life? Ponder one moment at a time. Close your eyes and look around at the scene in your imagination. Are there any important objects involved?
* Think of the **places** you have frequented over the years—your favorite coffee shops, museums, markets, gardens. Do any objects come to mind when you visualize those places?
* If your house was on fire and you had to evacuate, what objects would you grab before running out the door?
* What are your most important **values** and **experiences**? What do you **love**? Are there objects that accompany these feelings, or stand for them metaphorically?

* What are the quintessential objects of your **childhood**? What objects helped form the person you are today?
* Which things in your life have **sentimental** value?
* Think about the important **people** of your life. Are there objects that remind you of them or your relationship with them over the years?
* Have you ever been sad over a **lost** or **broken** object? Can you think of anything you have that you would be crushed to lose or break? What objects in the world would you be **sad** to live without? Which make you **happy**?
* What objects do you **identify** with? Is there one that symbolizes who you are? What object could be your **mascot**?

IDEAS FOR MORE PROMPTS

Here is a list of the prompts scattered throughout the book, plus some new words that might be especially relevant for various characters you choose to portray. A diverse range of emotions, object types, times of life, etc., makes for a rich vignette. Write them into the empty boxes, swap them in for words that are already there, or peruse them to spark ideas. You can also use these prompts when interviewing someone in person.

mystery	travel	handmade	emotional	afternoon
habit	funny	romance	flavorful	furniture
good memories	well made	hobby	necessary	aid
best ever	broken	first time	work of art	what if
sentimental	fixed	surprise	loved one	midnight
reminder	vintage	metaphor	dreamy	homemade
gift	antique	tool	inspiration	passage of time
someday	ancient	lots and lots	potential	hometown
nature	indulgence	new	a good time	fragile
well loved	goal	on the bus	experiment	longing
difficult	serious	delight	sacred	strange

accomplished
favorite book
essential
warm
freedom
ponder
childhood
heirloom
guide
lost and found
kindness
bedtime
solitary
journey
exercise
Sunday morning
lucky
fall
winter
summer
spring
home
scent
far away
splurge
hand-me-down
hilarious
plastic
cold
hidden
risk
independence
family
clothing / shoes
tradition
precious
foreign
worn
pleasure
daring
companion
again and again

favorite
playful
infinite
practice
simple
mass-produced
future
love / hate
urban
symbol
exotic
from a book
taste
photograph
a long time ago
heavenly
remarkable
work
calm
identity
extra special
metal
awe
grief
wonder
strong
lost
kitchen
soulful
dedication
earthy
love
ceremony
knowledge
rural
reminisce
big
type of flower
type of plant
animal
insect
sound

helpful
scary
delicious
utensil
a great idea
old
poetic
inherited
borrowed
textured
elegant
Saturday afternoon
mind
body
learn
communication device
ritual
colorful
nostalgic
beautiful
wooden
contemplate
encourage
accomplishment
inner self
generous
magical
treasured
festive
dream
unique
for hours and hours
truth
leisure
courage
mentor
catalyst
adventure
wish
heartbreak

sad
grow
change
passion
underappreciated
small
unknown origin
endearing
challenging
shock
game
always
absurd
holiday
daydream
past
vehicle
mascot
creative
philosophical
spiritual
musical instrument
long lost
careful
compassion
talent
lesson
daily
magnificent
trust
wonderful
bliss
friendship
cooking
amusement
relaxation
brilliant
confusing
tired
unbelievable
endless
museum piece

trusty
treat
in the car
curiosity
collection
sleepy
power
hope
lovely
heavy
glass
rusty
zeal
important
community
possibility
insight
technology
influence
care
heal
powerful
tend
skill
Friday night
gadget
food / beverage
accessory
toy
sport
often
empathy
ridiculous
imagine
waking up
snack
joke
only once
reunited
thrift store
celebration
social

STORY ARCHIVE

Objects carry stories. This story archive is a place for the memories and musings sparked by some of the objects you collect into your vignettes. Some objects speak for themselves; others acquire meaning through the telling and retelling of stories.

object: RADIO
story: AS A CHILD, MY MOM WOULD TUCK HER DAD'S RADIO UNDER HER PILLOW AT BEDTIME AND LISTEN WHILE FALLING ASLEEP.

object: PENCILS
story: THOREAU GREW UP WORKING IN HIS FAMILY'S PENCIL-MAKING BUSINESS. THIS SEEMS ESPECIALLY FITTING CONSIDERING HIS EVENTUAL PASSION FOR BOTH WRITING AND THE WOODS.

object: RAINCOAT + HAT
story: BASHO'S RAINGEAR WAS HANDWOVEN OUT OF RICE STRAW!

object: BACKGAMMON GAME
story: CHARLES DARWIN AND HIS WIFE, EMMA, PLAYED BACKGAMMON EVERY EVENING. EMMA USUALLY WON.

object: WATERCOLOR PAINT SET
story: I GREW UP IN A HOUSE FULL OF ART SUPPLIES. I WAS UNSTOPPABLY ENAMORED WITH THEM FROM THE GET-GO. BUT IT'S NOT JUST A COINCIDENCE THAT MY CHILDHOOD HOME OFFERED ALL THESE THINGS. IT'S ALSO THAT MY MOTHER PROVIDED THEM PRECISELY BECAUSE SHE NOTICED HOW MUCH I LOVED THEM. THANKS, MOM!

object: PICNIC BASKET
story: EMILY DICKINSON WOULD PUT BAKED GOODS AND POEMS IN HER PICNIC BASKET, TIE A CORD ONTO THE HANDLE, AND LOWER IT DOWN TO THE CHILDREN BELOW HER BEDROOM WINDOW.

object: ....

story: ....

....

....

....

....

....

object: ....

story: ....

....

....

....

object: ....

story: ....

....

....

....

object: ....

story: ....

....

....

....

object: ....

story: ....

....

....

....

....

....

....

....

....

object: ....

story: ....

....

....

....

....

....

....

....

....

object: ....
story: ....
....
....
....
....

object: ....
story: ....
....
....
....
....

object: ....
story: ....
....
....
....
....

object: ....
story: ....
....
....
....

object: ....
story: ....
....
....

object: ....
story: ....
....
....

object: ....
story: ....
....
....
....
....

object: ....
story: ....
....
....
....
....
....
....
....

object: ....

story: ....

....

....

....

....

....

object: ....

story: ....

....

....

....

object: ....

story: ....

....

....

....

object: ....

story: ....

....

....

....

object: ....

story: ....

....

....

....

....

....

....

....

....

object: ....

story: ....

....

....

....

....

....

....

....

....

object: ....

story: ....

....

....

....

....

object: ....

story: ....

....

....

....

....

object: ....

story: ....

....

....

....

....

object: ....

story: ....

....

....

....

object: ....

story: ....

....

....

object: ....

story: ....

....

....

object: ....

story: ....

....

....

....

....

object: ....

story: ....

....

....

....

....

....

....

....

....

....

object: ....

story: ....

....

....

....

....

object: ....

story: ....

....

....

....

object: ....

story: ....

....

....

....

object: ....

story: ....

....

....

....

object: ....

story: ....

....

....

....

....

....

....

....

....

object: ....

story: ....

....

....

....

....

....

....

....

....

object: ....
story: ....
....
....
....
....

object: ....
story: ....
....
....
....
....

object: ....
story: ....
....
....
....
....

object: ....
story: ....
....
....
....

object: ....
story: ....
....
....

object: ....
story: ....
....
....

object: ....
story: ....
....
....
....
....

object: ....
story: ....
....
....
....
....
....
....
....
....

object: ....

story: ....

....

....

....

....

object: ....

story: ....

....

....

....

object: ....

story: ....

....

....

....

object: ....

story: ....

....

....

....

object: ....

story: ....

....

....

....

....

....

....

....

....

object: ....

story: ....

....

....

....

....

....

....

....

....

ACKNOWLEDGMENTS

To My Editor—

Thank you, Meg, for believing in this book and going out on a limb with me. I was pleasantly astonished when you told me to just trust my instincts and make the book that only I could make. You have provided a beautiful bento box and I have poured my heart into it. Working with you has been a true delight.

ABOUT THE AUTHOR

Lea Redmond is always looking for the poem hiding inside of things: a saltshaker, a clothes tag, a hand gesture, a cloud. She is infinitely intrigued by the way experiences can slip from the ordinary to the extraordinary, and she endeavors to make things that hold this possibility. Lea's World's Smallest Post Service has charmed thousands with its tiny letters. She designs whimsical knitting patterns for *Knit the Sky*, also the title of an upcoming book. Her journal series, including *Letters to My Future Self* and *Letters to My Baby*, are much loved. When she's not hiking in the woods or wandering through junk shops, she's working and playing at Leafcutter Designs, her creative studio in Berkeley, California. You're invited to join her at leafcutterdesigns.com, where you can send tiny mail, download knitting patterns, participate in creative projects, and order playful goods. Lea would love to hear from you!

leafcutterdesigns.com
@LeafcutterAnt on Twitter
Leafcutter on Instagram